MW01130098

The Pinecone Walk

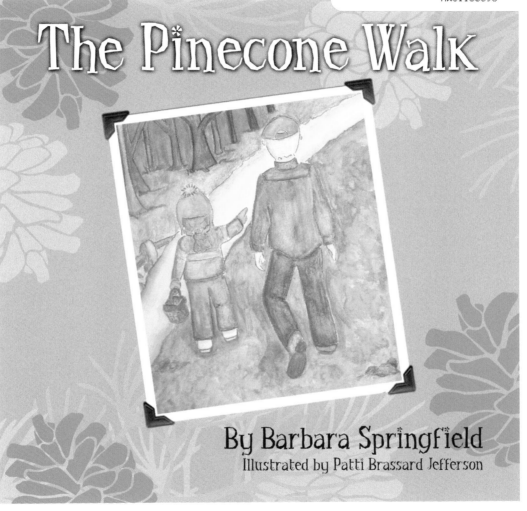

By Barbara Springfield
Illustrated by Patti Brassard Jefferson

Halo ●●●●
Publishing International

Look for treasures everyday!

Barbara Springfield

ISBN 13: 978-1-61244-319-5
Library of Congress Control Number: 2014909484

Printed in the United States of America

Halo Publishing International
www.halopublishing.com

Published by Halo Publishing International
1100 NW Loop 410
Suite 700 - 176
San Antonio, Texas 78213
Toll Free 1-877-705-9647
www.halopublishing.com
www.holapublishing.com
e-mail: contact@halopublishing.com

This book is dedicated to my husband, Jonny, who walks beside me each day as we discover life's treasures. And to my Mom, who showed me the beauty of Nature from the very beginning.

My grandfather said to me, "Let's go on a pinecone walk.
We will look for treasures as we go, keeping quiet we must not talk."

We bundled into our jackets and pushed our hats down tight.
We pulled on our boots, opened the door, and stepped out into the morning light.

5

And we walked on.

We walked along quietly not making a sound.
The first treasures we found were right on the ground.

Tracks made by an early morning deer.
Probably heard us and ran out of fear.

A stick that looked like an old man's cane.

A stone washed clean by yesterday's rain.

And we walked on.

The next treasure was something to hear and to spy: the sound of a red-tailed hawk swooping nearby.

And then we found beside the trail,

a long ago turtle had left its shell.

And we walked on.

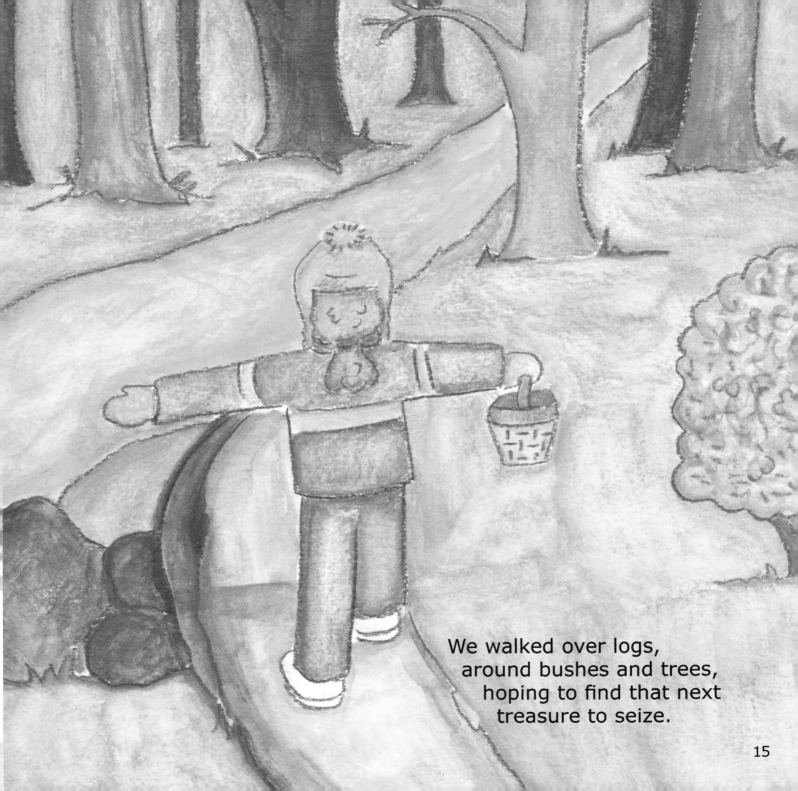

We walked over logs,
around bushes and trees,
hoping to find that next
treasure to seize.

It wasn't long before we
heard way up high, the
chattering of squirrels
as they rushed by.

16

They were searching for their hidden treasure, nuts and corn; some were still sleeping on this very cold morn.

And we walked on.

And there on the path that the wind had blown by lay an abandoned bird nest made out of horsehair and rye.

The next treasure we found was a feather so light.
It had fallen from a bird in flight.
I took off my hat and stuck it in my hair.

Grandfather said,
"You should
leave it there."

And we walked on.

It wasn't long before we could tell
the next treasure was a wonderful smell.

The smell of pine trees as they stood along the pond
and the pine straw carpet that our boots walked on.

And there they were!
Pinecones...pinecones...
EVERYWHERE!
Big ones and small ones...
enough for the forest to share.

We gathered them in our basket and carried them home that day, keeping all the treasures we had found on our way.

And as we sat in our kitchen that night, beside the stove that our pinecones helped light, we remembered the sights we had seen on our way.

24

But, to me, the very best treasure was being with my grandfather that day!

CPSIA information can be obtained
at www.ICGtesting.com
Printed in the USA
BVIC01n0146231014
371181BV00004B/2